Finding My Life Through The Children's Home

by Janet Louise Mancini

Daniel Webster quote
1782-1852

If we work upon marble, it will perish,
If we work upon brass, time will efface it.
If we rear temples, they will crumble into dust
but if we work upon immortal minds and install into them
just principles, we are then engraving that upon tablets which
no time will efface, but will brighten and brighten to all eternity.

Acknowledgments

There are countless individuals I have to thank for being a part of this research. I don't know where to begin. I have made many, many friends along the way. I have been given so much help in putting this together. From the first time I stepped back into The Children's Home, I had no idea what I would find. I was looking for information about my birth mother. I felt this was the grieving process for my birth mother. Grief sometimes takes a lifetime. Grief can also heal the soul.

Thanks goes to my birth mother, Mary Margaret Morris-Lener
my adopted parents, Alberta and Baptiste Mancini
Workers in The Children's Home
Lewana Gordon- King, Helen Gordon-Fike, Catherine Holland (Curator of the PA Room, Uniontown library) Vicki Leonelli
Roger Victor
Pamela Collins
James Stambaugh
Sandy McGill
The Fayette County Children's Aid Society
The Fayette County Genealogy Project
Fayette County Yahoo Group, their countless hours of research for documents that helped me   put my life together
The Fayette County Children and Youth Service, David Madison
The Free Methodist Church, Pastor James Jobes, Uniontown, PA.

Also thanks goes to all the contacts from the children that lived in The Children's Home. I will never forget what you have done for me. All our life stories are alike and this is what binds us together as a family.

Finding My Life Through The Children's Home

My reason for writing this history is because I want to help make someone else's search easier than mine was.

Not only was I able to find pictures and articles about the history of The Children's Home, but I also found my biological family, which I never knew I had. As strange as that sounds, that is what happened.

You see, I am an adopted child. It was at the request of our mother, Mary Margaret Morris-Lener, that my twin brother John and I be placed in The Children's Home. The Children's Home was located at 141 Oakland Avenue, Uniontown, PA. Our birth mother died a few days after placing us there. We went to live at the home in June of 1957.

The Legacy of The Adopted Child
Author Unknown

Once there were two women who never knew each other,
One you do not remember the other you call mother.
Two different lives shaped to make you one,
One became your guiding star,
The other became your sun.
The first one gave you life,
And the second taught you to live it.
The first one gave you a need for love,
The second was there to give it.
One gave you a nationality,
The other gave you a name.
One gave you a talent,
The other gave you aim.
One gave you emotions,
The other calmed your fears,
One saw your first sweet smile,
The other dried your tears.
One sought for you a home that she could not provide,
The other prayed for a child and her hope was not denied.
And now you ask me through your tears,
The age old question unanswered through the years,
Heredity or environment which are you a product of?
Neither, my darling neither,
Just two different kinds of love.

John, Baptiste Mancini, and Janet

Our adopted parents were Alberta and Baptiste Mancini. We were placed in my adopted home on Memorial Day 1958. Our adoption was finalized on Christmas Eve 1958. Our parents were looking to adopt a little boy, but when they came to The Children's Home and found out there were twins they did not want to separate us, they wanted both of us. This makes the biggest difference in the life of a child.

I had the best of everything but most of all was their love and acceptance. I thank God every day for the life I was blessed with.

I wanted to add here, the woman who had lived in the house beside my parents' home, Dona Sands, told my parents that there was a Children's Home that was closing and the children needed to be placed. It was Dona Sands' aunt, Mary McKnight-Connelly, who was the matron of the home.

Then after many visits from The Children's Aid Society to my parents' home, they were found very worthy of children.

After the death of my adopted mother, I became curious about my birth mother. This was August 2000. My brother John had done some searching years earlier, but now my time has come. John gave me my birth mother's name and my search began.

I called an old friend of my adopted mother, Dona Sands, and

3

ask her if she knew where The Children's Home was located. Dona wasn't sure, but knew it was in Fayette County, PA. It turns out Dona was the niece of the Matron of The Children's Home, Mary McKnight-Connelly. I called the Uniontown Library, and spoke to a woman who told me the building at 141 Oakland Avenue, Uniontown, was still there. This event transpired 45 years after leaving The Children's Home.

The following week, I went back to the building, and as I walked the floors and looked all around, I was amazed because memories started to flow like water. I recognized the black and white linoleum, the large oak stairway, the two large dining rooms, and the scenery. I realized this was the first day of my life that I could remember, Memorial Day, 1958, the day my twin brother John and I left The Children's Home. As we were leaving with my our new parents, Alberta and Baptiste Mancini, the sun was shining brightly through the Poplar trees, and I felt such a warmth and comfort from the sun that I knew everything would be alright. As the sun came through the trees and windows of the car, I was fascinated by this feeling and sight.

I will never forget that drive to our new home. A place where I felt very much loved and accepted. After having lost my birth mother, birth father, all my siblings, and enduring a life-threatening scalding accident at 2 years of age, I was ready to go on with my life. I was very happy in my new home.

While visiting there, I saw three large photo copies of The Children's Home and ask if anyone knew who the woman was in the photo. I later found out that the woman in the photos was Mary McKnight-Connelly, the Matron of The Children's Home.

I wanted to be informed if anyone came by that either worked or lived in the home, or was a child there when I was. The building had become The Easter Seals Office, and I left my name and number at the desk, hoping to make a connection. After a week, I could wait no longer, so I called and was told there was a woman and a man there taking a video of the place earlier that week. It turns out the woman was Lewana Gordon-King, who was a helper with the boys at the home and the man was Gary Wilson. He had

4

been a child there when I was. I was so excited I could not wait. I was given Lewana's phone number and I called her. She ask me three questions:

1) Do you have natural curly blond hair? I said yes
2) Do you have a twin brother named John? I said yes
3) Do you have scar on your left shoulder? I said yes

I immediately felt chills run up and down my arms, and the hair stood up on them. Lewana than said "You're the Lener twins."

That is the first I heard my name. It is almost like I heard a echo sound.

It has taken awhile for that to set in.

I knew at this very moment that I had made a connection, and this was my proof. I knew now that I could piece my life together.

Me, Helen Gordon-Fike, Lewana Gordon-King, John Mancini

I met Lewana Gordon-King, Helen Gordon-Fike and Catherine Holland on 01-10-2001, my birthday, 47 years after I left The Children's Home. These are the women who took care of me in The Children's Home. When I met them I felt as though they were mothers to me. They had taken many photos of John and I living at The Children's Home. I had never seen myself at 4 years of age and I was just fascinated at what I looked like. I could not take my eyes off of the photos for the longest time. I was very overwhelmed by the love and care these women had and still have for the children that lived at the home.

We lived together just like a family. We ate, slept, went to church and school together, just like a family. The place was exceptionally clean and we had very nutritious meals. The home would be visited periodically and unannounced by The Children's Aid Society. Some of the food was provided by The County Home and also DeCarlo's Greenhouse that provided vegetables for the home. There was even a local bakery that provided birthday cakes for all the children. We were well feed and very happy. At the time I lived at the home about 30 children lived there also. Ranging in age from months old to about 13 years of age.

Most of us attended The Free Methodist Church at 301 Evans St. in Uniontown, PA. But others attended the church their families were from. We attended the Boyle School that was located at 115 Downer Ave. Uniontown, PA.

I got my mother's date of death from The Fayette County Children and Youth service. I was able to get a copy of my proposed adoption papers which I had never seen. This opened up a whole new world to me. During the 1950's all adoption records were sealed because of privacy reasons. It was in the best interest of the child to be protected. In my case it was the right thing to do, since I was so young. In order to receive my records now, I had to show my adopted birth certificate and my drivers license and, as an adopted child, I needed proper ID.

Once I did get my records, I had found out a lot of information on my birth mother. It had her date of death. I was then able to look for her obituary. And it stated that there were 9 children in the family. I was in complete shock and even more of a shock was to see my name in her obituary. In reading it I found out I had lost one sister to Pneumonia at 9 months of age. And as I was reading about my mother's siblings I started to wonder if she had any still living. Well she had a sister left, and her name was Catherine Nutt.

I gave Catherine a call and told her who I was. She was just as

6

shocked as I was to hear from me. We talked for quite awhile and planned to meet the next week. When I walked into the house she said, "Oh my God!" It was just like her sister walking through the door. She said "You look just like your mother." Aunt Catherine gave me my first picture of my birth mother and every time I look at it I get chills. I look exactly like her.

I have the same smile, eyes, natural curly hair and hands. I could not stop looking at her photo. I am amazed.

Aunt Catherine knew where my oldest and youngest sisters were living. I was able to meet my youngest sister, Eleanor that day. She was so excited; I was so overwhelmed. I now had 7 more siblings. My brothers and sisters have been looking for John and I all their lives. They never knew if we were separated or stayed together. It was the best thing for us to be adopted together.

My siblings and I are getting to know one another by emails, texting, visits and phone calls. We now have a lifetime to talk about. I ended up finding four sisters and three brothers. What a blessing it has been.

My adopted parents, Baptiste and Alberta Mancini.

7

If anyone may have a connection to The Children's Home I can be contacted at oaklandave141@yahoo.com

Janet L. Mancine

Reunion of Brothers & Sisters - 2003
After 50 years of separation.

Me & Rose Hale (sister)

Robert Lener (brother) & Me

Eleanor Shipley (sister) & Me

Me, Mary Morris-Verbus (sister) & John Mancini

John Mancini, James Allamon (brother) & Me

Me, Bill Lener (brother) & John Mancini

11

Christmas Together: Family Separated as Children Reunites After Decades

Newspaper Articles

Taken from The Herald Standard, Sunday, December 22, 2002

This is a success story in more ways then one. We have come together as a family again. I now want to learn all I can about my siblings after we were separated, said Janet.

The women, who are natives of Fayette County, hope their story of long-lost siblings will encourage others in similar situations. In September, Janet discovered six brothers and sisters she never knew she had, while her siblings found Janet and her twin brother John, for whom they had been searching for years.

"As far as I am concerned , they could not have given me a better gift," said Eleanor. "And here I am, all of a sudden, I have all these relatives, " states Janet.

The siblings , nine altogether, lived in Oliver, North Union Township, as the children of Mary Margaret Morris-Lener and William Joseph Lener. Their mother, who suffered poor health, died in 1957 at the age of 39. Their father felt unable to care for the children after the death of his wife. The children were raised and/or adopted by various families. Their father died in 1984 from bone cancer. He was 68 years old.

The siblings, nine altogether, using their present names, are: Mary Elizabeth Morris-Verbus, 61; Rose Manila Grace Hale, 58 of Collinsville, VA; William Smith Lener, 57 of Aspers, PA; Robert Ellsworth Lener, 54 of Eden, NC; James Albert Allamon, 50 of Tacoma Park, MD; twins, Janet Louise Mancini, 49 of Monongahela, PA and John Edward Mancini, 49 of Albuquerque, NM; and Eleanor Mae Shipley, 48 of New Salem, PA.

A sister, Blanche Glendora Lener, 9 months of age of Uniontown, PA, passed away in 1948.

Eleanor, who was 3 years old when her mother died, was

12

adopted by Paul and Ethel Dahl of Hopwood. James was adopted by Gladys and Robert Allamon of Little Brownfield. Mary was raised by her grandparents, Albert and Rose Morris, who lived next door to the Leners' family home. Rose was raised by their Aunt Katie and Uncle Clarence Nutt in Oliver. Bobby and Billy went back and fourth between the Allamons, their father, and Aunt Isabelle and uncle Smith Lener of Uniontown.

In 1970, Eleanor, who knew she was adopted, decided to search for her brothers and sisters. But she did not actually pursue her quest until 1972 when she graduated from high school. She came in touch with her birth relatives. One adopted aunt knew a birth aunt. The birth aunt had Bobby's address, and Bobby had the address of their other siblings, except for Janet and John. The others had kept in touch.

Eleanor, who said she had decided to give up her search for the twins a week before finding Janet, said of the meeting, "It was like closing a hole in my heart."

Janet said, "For me, it was a completeness. Everything came together like a puzzle."

Eleanor wrote a "Why I Am Thankful" letter to the Herald Standard in November because of her joy in finding Janet and John. It read in part:

"Unless you have lived through a family that has been shattered by death and separated to all points of the earth, do you truly appreciate and are thankful when you get a phone call and it is a lost loved one on the other end of the phone. If anyone is truly thankful for friends and family, it is my brothers, sisters and myself."

In the interview, Eleanor said, "We believe this is our way of helping other people, so they won't get discouraged - they'll have hope. Said Janet, "Never give up hope. Whenever you come to a dead end, there's always a way around it. There's always a paper trail. You just have to look."

Family reunion

Black Diamond woman locates siblings separated in childhood

Twins John and Janet Mancini were four years old when they were placed in The Children's Home, Uniontown, a few days after the death of their mother, Mary Lener, in 1957. She was just 39 when she died.

Janet, who describes herself as the "bonus package," says they were adopted a year later by very loving parents, Alberta and Baptiste Mancini of Black Diamond.

"They had met in Charleroi when my mother worked for the Woodward family and settled in Black Diamond after their marriage," Janet Mancini says. "They learned of The Children's Home and went there to adopt a little boy. When they found there was a twin sister, they decided to take us both."

Janet, who still lives in the family home, said she decided to search for information about her biological mother and siblings after the death of her adoptive mother in August 2000.

"I thank God from the bottom of my heart to have had the most wonderful parents any child could ever need," she said. "I have felt His love through my parents."

She said she started the search for biological kin as part of her healing process. Her twin brother had moved to Albuquerque, N.M., 25 years earlier.

Janet Mancini met with phenomenal success.

She and John have seen their six surviving siblings and hope to hold a reunion with everyone together real soon.

William and Mary Margaret Lener of Oliver, North Union Township, had nine children; a girl named Blanche, died in infancy in 1948. In addition to the twins, the others are: Mary Elizabeth Verbus, Uniontown;

Rose Hale, Collinsville, Va.; William Lener, Aspen, Pa.; Robert Lener, Eden, N.C.; James Allamon, Tacoma Park, Md., and Eleanor Rosenberg, Bruceton Mills, West Va.

Eleanor, who was just 3 years old when their mother died, was adopted by Gladys and Robert Allamon of Little Brownfield almost immediately. Maternal grandparents Albert and Rose Morris raised Mary and an aunt and uncle, Katie and Clarence Nutt, took Rose into their home. Bobby and Billy went back and forth between their father, the Allamons and an aunt and uncle, Isabel and Smith Lener. Their father died in 1984.

Through contact with the Uniontown Public Library, Janet Mancini learned the address of The Children's Home. The building was later used by the Easter Seal Society after the children's home ceased operating in 1958.

She visited the site in October 2001 and asked for information on anyone known to have worked at The Children's Home. A week later she was put in touch with Lewana King who remembered Janet and even identified a scar on her shoulder, received in a childhood accident.

On her birthday, Jan. 16, Janet met with King, a resident of Farmington; her sister, Helen Fike, and Carolyn Hall, both of Uniontown. All three had worked at The Children's Home 45 years ago and provided Janet with many photos of her and John taken at the residence.

Viewing the pictures, Janet recalled the square block tile on the floor, the rows of cribs and beds and even a stair railing they used between

Emma Jene Lelik/For The Valley Independent
SIBLINGS FOUND – Janet Mancini of Black Diamond looks over the collection of family photographs. She located siblings separated 45 years ago.

floors.

"They had papers from May 1932 with information on the home," she said. "A little white Bible from the place indicates it was the first children's home in Fayette County."

The house on Oakland Avenue in Uniontown was built in 1889 and purchased in 1905 by coal baron J.V. Thompson who added it to his Oak Hill Estate as living quarters for his employees. It later became a foster home for children.

Janet Mancini continued her quest and, learning the records from The Children's Home had been turned over to Fayette County Children and Youth, she contacted them to find records of her mother's grave. She returned to the library and searched for her mother's obituary, having learned the date of her death at the cemetery. Through this document she found her mother had a sister, Catherine Nutt, surviving and Janet was able to meet with her also. The aunt assured her she looked "exactly like her mother."

At the cemetery she found the marker for her infant sister's grave and had a heart-shaped memorial stone placed at the site.

Mary Verbus gave Janet their mother's Bible that had all the births properly recorded in it.

"It was fortunate she gave it to me when she did," Janet said, "because her home later burned and all the contents were lost."

Janet, who works in the emergency room registration department at Mon Valley Hospital, is eager for a reunion when all the brothers and sisters will be together at one time.

EMMA JENE LELIK

Fayette County Children & Youth Services

When I went to FCYS, this is the type of information I was given.

Being I was adopted, I had to take my drivers license and my adopted birth certificate for proof of identity.

Fayette County Children & Youth Service
130 Old New Salem Road
Uniontown, PA 15401
724-430-1283

ᕐ March 1, 2002

Enclosed is a summary of your family background information, which we are able to share with you.

The information in your file was very limited. We found no birth or health information pertaining to you, except what is noted in the summary. We hope this information is helpful to you in your search for other family members.

Sincerely, Caseworker II

Summary Regarding Janet, DOB: 01-10-53

Janet was born to parents of the Caucasian race. The family descent is unknown. It is also unknown whether or not the birth parents graduated from high school. Both birth parents were of the Protestant faith as were the children. The biological mother gave birth to seven children. After the birth of her fourth child, it is reported she had an emotional breakdown. She apparently recovered and assumed her parental responsibilities as the husband took care of the children. She later gave birth to three more children, which included a set of twins. It is noted that the birth father worked as a laborer in a steel mill. The limited family history noted that the birth father's work history was limited. The family was on assistance. It was also noted that he drank excessively and was physically aggressive with his wife and oldest child (female). According to the information, he served time in jail. Janet is the third youngest of seven children born to her birth parents. Janet is also the sibling of a male twin. Janet's birth mother was 35 years old and the birth father was age 36 when she was born. The birth parents had one more daughter about a year and a half after the twins were born. The parents separated after the birth of the youngest child and had not lived together for sometime. The birth mother had apparently become ill (unknown, as source of illness was not mentioned). A few days before the birth mother's death, (twins were being cared for by the maternal grandparents), the birth mother requested that the Children's Aid Home look after the twins. She wanted them to have a good life and felt that they deserved a chance in life with a good family. The birth mother died at age 39 years. Janet and her twin brother John were approximately 4 years old at the time of her death. On June 19, 1957, Janet and her sibling were placed in the Children's Aid Home. Most of the remaining children were with relatives. Janet, along with her twin, was placed in an adoptive home on Memorial Day, May 31, 1958. They were adopted on Christmas Eve, December 24, 1958. Janet's physician gave her a physical examination and tests prior to the adoption. She was found to be physically fit. Janet was described as a healthy, good-looking child. We have no additional information, including health information regarding Janet.

Submitted by Caseworker II.

Proposed Adoption of Janet Lee and John Edward Lener (Twins)
Report of Investigation of Child Placement

Orphans' Court of Fayette County, Pennsylvania - Adoption completed December 24, 1958
before Judge Anderson, Washington County, Washington, PA - Attorney Clyde Tempest of
Monongahela, PA

To the Honorable, the Judge of said court: The undersigned respectfully reports as follows:
1. State full names of proposed adopters:
Albert Raymond Mancini and Baptiste Mancini
2. State actual place of residence of proposed adopters (city, borough, or township) and also give
other places of residence for at least five years last past.
707 Chestnut St. Monongahela, Washington County, PA. Lived at present address 9 years.
3. State post office address of adopters:
Monongahela, PA
4. State ages, places of birth, color and religion affiliation of adopters:
Alberta Raymond Mancini - born 09-18-1823, Uniontown, PA - white - Protestant,
Baptiste Mancini - born 01-05-1919, Monongahela - white - Protestant.
5. State date and place of marriage of adopters, state if either was previously married and, if so,
state cause of dissolution, whether by death or divorce.
Married 04-17-1949, Uniontown, PA, no previous marriages.
6. State names, ages and places of residence of all children of adopters, whether by this or by a
previous marriage or by adoptions.
No other children

7. State whether proposed adopters own their own home or rent the same. Describe briefly the
home as to physical characteristics, state of repair, number of rooms and furnishings. Give
names of all persons who reside in the home.
Own their home - 7 rooms - 2 baths - brick - good repair - nicely furnished. No others living in
the home.
8. State name and address of employer.
Self employed for 15 years.
9. Describe the appearance of adopters as to health and state if either has consulted a physician
during the last two years last past.
Very healthy looking couple. Have regular physical examinations.
10. State whether proposed adopters or either of them have ever been convicted of a crime and, if
so give date and circumstances.
Never
11. State the names and addresses of at least two well known persons who are well acquainted
with adopters and who may vouch for their moral character, industry and good reputation in the
community.
Joseph Radius - Monongahela, PA
William McKnight - Uniontown, PA
Dona Sands - Monongahela, PA
Mildred Tempest - Monongahela, PA
12. State the full name, color, date and place of birth and religious affiliation of the child.
Janet Lee Lener - 1-10-1953, Uniontown, PA. White - Protestant
John Edward Lener - 01-10-1953 Uniontown, PA White - Protestant.
13. Mancinis had made application for child upon investigation. They were found to be worthy
in all respects to assume responsibility of these children and were place on May 31, 1958.

18

(Memorial Day)

14. Give the name and address of intermediary, if any.

Children's Aid Society of Fayette County, Uniontown, PA

15. State whether or not a physical or mental examination of the child has been made by a
competent person if so, give details.

Dr. John D. Sturgeon, Uniontown, pediatrician has examined both children and they are in good
physical condition. IQ tests given by Glenn Irvine and they are mentally fit.

16. Describe the general appearance of the child as to health.

Healthy good looking children.

17. State the names, ages, color, places of residence and religious affiliation of the natural parents
of the child. Describe briefly their moral and social standards.

Mother died 06-13-1957, born in Smock, PA, 02-20-1918. White - Protestant

Father born in Dunbar, PA 01-28-1916 - White Protestant.

Morals questionable - mother better than father, who never kept family and whose moral and
social standards are very low.

18. State whether or not any money consideration was paid or promised to be paid by the
proposed adopters or either of them to the natural parents, to the physician or to any other person
in order to procure possession of the child.

None

19. State reasons natural parents surrendered possession of the child.

Parents had not lived together for some time. Father never worked. Drank and abused family.
Was in jail several times. Family had been on public assistance for years. After the mother died,
the maternal grandparents placed the younger children for adoption. The twins in The Children's
Home. Grandparents were not able to care for these children. Older

Lener children had been in
Children's home for some time previous to the birth of the twins.
Father never contributed to
their support and they were placed for adoption.
20. State reasons given by adopters for proposed adoption of the child and whether other
members of the family, if any, are agreeable.
Adopters can have no children of their own. There are no other members of the family.
21. State any additional facts pertinent to this investigation.

A few days before she died, the mother requested the Children's Aid Society look after her
children after she was gone. The children have a good IQ and deserve the chance in life which
their foster parents are able to give them.

Respectfully submitted,

Elizabeth B. Jeffrey
Children's Aid Society

Name of Child (Record)

Admitted June 19, 1957 - Janet and John Lener (Twins)
Born January 10, 1953

Admitted by Grandfather on Mother's side (Albert Morris and
Aunt Catherine Morris)
Janet and John Lener were placed on May 31, 1958 with Mrs.
Albert Raymond and Mr. Baptiste
Mancini - address as 707 Chestnut Street - Monongahela,
Washington County, Pennsylvania.
The twins were adopted on December 24, 1958 to Mr. and Mrs.
Baptiste Mancini in Washington
county Court before Judge Anderson of Washington, Pennsylvania.

Older photos from The Children's Home

The Workers of The Children's Home

Mary McKnight-Connelly, Matron; Leona Glass, nurse; Lulu Sickles

Lewana Gordon-King - Christmas 1956

22

Bertha Spaw - cook's helper - 1957

Mary McKnight-Connelly
Matron of The Children's Home - 1957

23

Lewana Gordon-King - Boy's helper

Catherine Holland - Playroom/girl's helper; Ruth Hutzel - Assistant Cook; Mary Bednar - Nursery/Head girl; Lewana Gordon-King - Laundry/Boy's helper; Mary McKnight-Connelly - Matron - 1957

24

Going home - Mary Bednar - Head Nursery

Lewana King - Laundry/Boy's helper,
Janet Kimmell - Helper as needed

Catherine Holland 1957 - Nursery girl
She loved the babies

Christmas at The Children's Home
Mrs. Jefferies, woman in the back, a long
time member of The Children's Aid Society

26

Front: Sara Romesburg, Mary Bednar,
Ruth Hutzel, Catherine Holland
Back: Mary Connelly, Peggy Wallace

Mary McKnight-Connelly, Matron,
helping the children on the merry-go-round - 1955

1957 - Lewana Gordon-King, Mary Bednar,
Katherine Holland, Mary McKnight-Connelly
Mrs. Hutzel

1957

28

1957 - Shirley Gordon - Nursery girl

Catherine Holland - Playroom and girl's room,
Mary Connelly (Matron) Mary Bednar (Head of
nursery room), Lewana Gordon-King
(Laundry and boys), Mrs. Hutzel (Asst.)

Catherine Holland (right), Mary Connelly
(Matron), Katherine Donna Connelly - 1956

Story time with Helen Gordon-Fike

1956 - Mrs. Hutzel, and
Mrs. Sarah Romesburg (seamstress

Mary Bednar

31

1956

Bath time at The Children's Home
Helen Gordon-Fike - Girl's helper

32

Bath time for the boys Lewana Gordon

On the Front Steps of The Children's Home

1958 - Easter

Front porch at The Children's Home - 1954

1956 - Play area in The Children's Home

34

Going to church (front porch)

Easter 1956 - Helen Gordon

35

Mrs. Helen Wilson - front steps - 1957

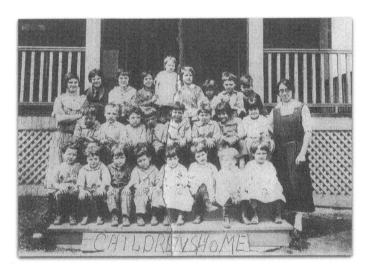

1920's - The Children's Home
141 Oakland Ave, Uniontown, PA

36

Inside The Children's Home

1956

1957 - Story time - Can you see the
beautiful nursery Rhyme murals?
They were done by local artists

Playtime - steps leading
to the attic. Notice how low the
railing is for the children

38

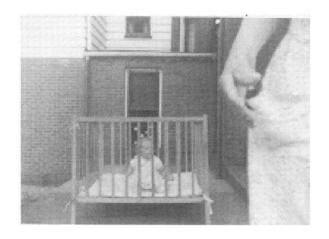

Rear of The Children's Home - playtime

Children's Playroom

Story time 1957

Playroom 1957

Helen Gordon-Fike,
Playroom/Girl's Helper - 1957

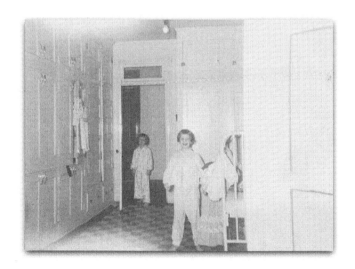

Ready for bed

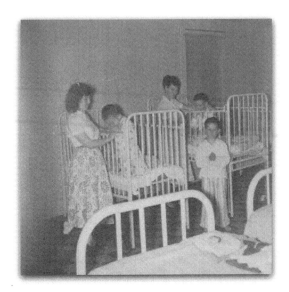

1958

1958

1958

All ready for bed - boy's room

Attic - where the women that work stayed

Not too happy - they want out!

Up early for Easter Baskets - 1954

45

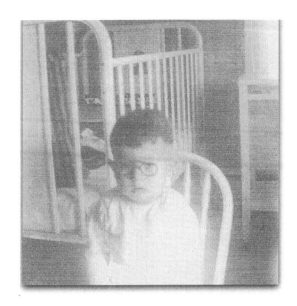

1957 - The boys' bedroom - This little one
does not look too happy, wants to stay up.

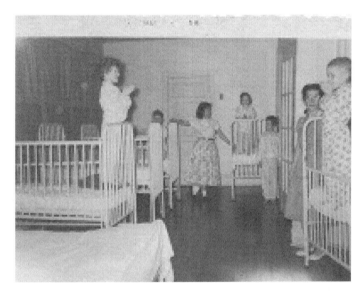

Girls Bedroom - bedtime - May, 1958

46

1956

Scout Troop #42 (Friday) – The Children's Home – The Herald Standard

47

1956

Vocational School Beauty Operators

The Harold Standard

The Children's Home, Highland Ave - 1916-1917

49

The Piano in the Front Room Was a Popular Place for Pictures in The Children's Home

July, 1958

Front room - ready for Sunday School

1956 - Front room

1956

51

The piano in the front room
was a great place for pictures

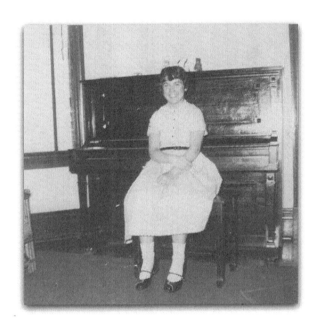

Twins - Janet & John (Johnny) Lener
Children's Home - May 1958

1958 - John & Janet Lener

53

1957

54

1958

1956

55

1958

1956

The Children's Home Was Full of Fun: Christmas, Birthdays, and Meals in the Dining Rooms

Christmas at The Children's Home - 1956

Christmas at The Children's Home - 1954

1956 - Christmas tree at The Children's Home
Uniontown, PA

Christmastime at The Children's Home 1957

1957 - Birthday Party

1957 - Some of the bibs were as large as us.

1957

Birthday Party - November 1958

Birthday Party - 1958

Children's Home - 1958

61

Having a snack in the dining room - 1958

1958

62

There were two large dining rooms at the home.
We ate a lot of nutritious meals here.

Christmastime at The Children's Home

The Jaycees would take the children on shopping trips

Outside The Children's Home

1956

Easter Egg Hunt - 1954

Covered Picnic Area

All dressed up for Sunday School

October 1958

A nice day to be outside playing and having fun 1953

Best friends - taken in picnic area

1954

Everyone set for a day out.

Catherine Holland (right) helps with girls

1954

The children would be picked up by
Panzara's bus to be taken to Sunday School

Coming home from church

1957

We were taught to help one another - 1956

72

1958

1956

1956 - Ready to go on the swing set

1956

1956

January 1957

1957

1956

1957

1956

1957

1957

1956

John and Janet with their friends
at The Children's Home - 1957

Enjoying a ride on the merry-go-round
Playground at The Children's Home - Sept 1957

Twins - John and Janet Lener - 1957

1957

The Children's Home, 141 Oakland Ave

The Children's Home - Jan 1958

83

1958

March 1958

84

1958

1958

Workers & children - May 25, 1958

Nov 1957 -- Covered picnic area

The children would be picked the children up
and taken to church

DeCarlo's Greenhouse

The children's Home - opened 1919 - closed 1958

Rear view of the Children's Home

90

1957 - Back view of the Children's Home

The children's Home
opened 1919 - closed 1958

91

And Then There was ...

My first picture of my birth mother,
Mary Margaret Morris-Lener

Janet Louise Lener-Mancini - 1957

My adopted mother
Alberta Raymond-Mancini

Adoption picture - 12-24–1958

My Life On a Daily Basis at The Children's Home
By Helen Gordon-Fike

I have always wanted to work with children. As a Sunday School teacher, I felt God had answered my prayer. When I was asked to work in The Children's Home, I made my home with them. I had the children ranging from age 3 to 12 years of age. We would always go to the learning room where they all studied and did many things to make their imaginations come alive. One particular memory I have, is we would get large packages of wallpaper and I would ask the children to cut out things that came to memory to make pictures with. The children loved this. I helped them with their lessons, read stories to the smaller ones and taught them Sunday School songs. I would walk the children to The Boyle School, which was only a few blocks away. We ate our meals together along with the staff, just like a family, took them to church on Sunday. They were happy children and were taught to care and share with one another. I cannot write all the things we have done and the happy times we have shared. In The Children's Home we tried to bring them up to trust the Lord and guide them in His ways. These children are men and women now and have found their way in the world. It has been many years since God Called me and blessed me in His service. I pray I have done some good. I am glad I was part of their lives as they have blessed mine. I have never forgotten them.

My Day at The Children's Home
by Lewana Gordon-King

Lewana Gordon-King

I started to work at The Children's Home in 1957 and was hired to do the laundry. I stayed at the home as all the others did. I slept on the 3rd floor along with my sister Helen. I would get up early and get myself ready for the day. Then I would go down to the second floor where the boys were and got them up, washed, dressed and ready for school. Then we would go down to the first floor to the dining room for breakfast. All the boys would then go to the playroom with Helen Gordon-Fike until time for school. I then went down to the basement to do the laundry for all the children and some of the workers.

We usually got one and a half days off a week, and when the nursery girl had her day off, I worked in the nursery. We all took turns when someone had a day off. We all worked together, and it made it a very nice and happy place to work.

We had quite a few workers, the Matron, cooks, seamstress, nursery lady, and the cleaning ladies. We helped each other and things went well, and we all loved the children. They were well taken care of.

Lewana (Gordon) King

97

My Life Working at The Children's Home

Catherine Holland started working at The Children's Home in 1954 and stayed until it closed in 1957. Her parents, Elizabeth & Ben Holland, would come and visit her while she worked there. Catherine was hired as a cleaning lady but also took care of the children in the nursery. She told me of an incident that happened one day when she was out sweeping the steps. Catherine said as she was sweeping she could hear the faint cry of a baby. When she tuned around she noticed there was a basket at the bottom of the steps. Here when she walked over to pick it up there was a baby boy in a basket. Someone who was not able to care for the child, brought him there to be taken care of. From that time on the baby's name became Bobby Oakland, named after Oakland Avenue the home sat on.

She told me many names of the matrons that had worked there including: Leona Glass and Mary McKnight- Connelly, who was the matron while she was there. Miss Hood and Mrs. Jeffrey's were the women on The Children's Aid Society who visited the home often to see how it was being run.

Description of The Children's Home

The annex was built on in 1952. On the lower floors you would find ten cribs, two adult size hospital beds, complete kitchen, nurses's room, hospital style sterilizer and a bathroom. On the upper floors the infant nursery, kitchen, bathroom and storage space. In the other parts of the home you would find the girls and boys bedrooms, play areas, two large dining rooms, living room, matron's quarters, isolation bedrooms. (Children were kept in isolation for two weeks when they came to the home before associating with any other children.) The yard consisted of shrubbery, flowers, playground, three swing sets, sand boxes, merry-go-round, and a covered porch for picnics. The storage area contained a place for the laundry room, furnace, a place for canning and a deep freezer.

So, as you go through this pictorial history, you will find what I have collected over the years. It has been a great enjoyment for myself. These photographs are the story of our lives.

Children's Aid Society Matrons and Members

The Daily News Standard
Prominent Uniontown Women Subscribe to Children's Aid Charter

Incorporation of the Children's Aid Society of Fayette County auxiliary of the Children's Aid Society of Western Pennsylvania is provided in a petition presented before the Fayette county courts Tuesday morning. Learning the signature of 33 of Uniontown's representative women. By it's assumption of broader duties in the case of little Fayette County Orphans through the splendid new home it has purchased on Oakland Avenue, the society felt the need for a more permanent foundation than that granted through the state parent body. The Society will have greater responsibility and will be able to assume all of the trusts allowed under law. The petition states the society has been formed to provide for destitute and neglected children

Catherine Holland started working at The Children's Home in 1954 and stayed until it closed in 1957. Her parents, Elizabeth & Ben Holland, would come and visit her while she worked there. Catherine was hired as a cleaning lady, but also took care of the children in the nursery. She told me of an incident that happened one day when she was out sweeping the steps.

Catherine said as she was sweeping, she could hear the faint cry of a baby. When she turned around, she noticed there was a basket at the bottom of the steps. When she walked over to pick it up, there was a baby boy in the basket. Someone who was not able to care for the child, brought him there to be taken care of. From that time on, the baby's name became Bobby Oakland, named after Oakland Avenue the home sat on.

She told me many names of the matrons that had worked there, including: Leona Glass and Mary McKnight-Connelly, who was the matron while she was there. Miss Hood and Mrs. Jeffrey were the women on The Children's Aid Society who visited the home often to see how it was being run.

Historical Facts on The Children's Home

1800 - The Children's Home was a break off of The Fayette County Home. The judges voted not to have any children living under the conditions at the Fayette County Home.

1915-1916 - First Children's Home located at the home of Mrs. W. E. Crow, she who was a member of the Children's Aid Society. 75 Highland Avenue, Uniontown, PA.

1917-1918 - Second Children's Home was located on 80 McClellandtown Road, Uniontown, PA

1919-1958 - Third Children's Home was located on 141 Oakland Avenue, Uniontown, PA. The home was dissolved in 1990.

The Children's Aid Society which was founded in 1887 and was reorganized and incorporated in by making a temporary home for them and later finding a permanent home through their adoption in some family. The cost of membership is $1.00 per year.

The number of directors is fixed as five and those serving the first year are: Mrs. Mary E. Hackney, Mrs. Emily R. Hess, Miss Mary E. Sturgeon, Mrs. Anna V. McShane and Mrs. Millie R. Bortz

Other subscribers to the petition are:
Mrs. Emma R. Rankin, Mrs. Mary T. Ewing, Mrs. Mary E. Eastman, M. Elizabeth Baily, Mary K. Johns, Mrs. Mary E. Hackney, Mrs. Lyde H. Hess, Mrs. Nellie G. Cline, Mrs. Rebecca Molans, Mrs. Jacob Davis, Mrs. Abe Cohan, Ada Curry Crow, Jennie Morrow Jones, Mrs. Millie R. Bortz, Mrs. Mary F. Barclay, Mrs. Anna Darby, Mrs. Frances M. Jones, Mrs. Julia H. Porter, Mrs. Izetta L. Evans, Mrs. Blanche E. Fowler, Mrs. Frank Ellis Evans, Mrs. Helen E. Hustead, Mrs. Nora A. Pickens, Mrs. Cora B. Smith, Mrs. H. G. Mansell, Mrs. J. G. Remington, Mrs. Iva Stewart Sparks, Mrs. Leora Armstrong Davidson, Mrs. Belle S. Cottom, and Mrs. Emma V. Whyel

Children's Aid Society of Pennsylvania

http://www.childrenshomepgh.org/lemieux-family-center

By permission of The Children's Home of Pittsburgh and Lemieux Family Center I wanted to share this site with you. I was overwhelmed by the love each worker there had for each child that entered the doors of this home. If you ever have the chance to visit, please do. It will change your life for the better.

Taken from Commonwealth of Pennsylvania Department of Welfare

County Manual of Child Welfare Services

1815 - Orphan Society of Philadelphia
1869 - State Board of Commissioners of Public Charities
1871 - Annual Report
1883 - Children's Aid Society of Pennsylvania
1909 - President Roosevelt called first White House conference on Children's Health
1912 - U. S. creates first Children's Bureau, First Annual Report by Julia Lathrop - Chief of Children's Bureau
1913 - Mother's Assistance Fund
1921 - Creation of the Department of Welfare Commonwealth of Pennsylvania
1923 - Children's Commission appointed
1933 - Juvenile Court Law revised: Magistrates and Aldermen may no longer commit children to Institutions under 16 years of age
1935 - Federal Social Security - First Annual report - Board of Commissioners - Public Charities of Pennsylvania 1871
1936 - Rural Extension Created within Department of Welfare
1937 - Pennsylvania passes General Assistance Laws
1938 - Child Welfare Unit - Rural Extension Unit and federal funds

Family Services of Western Pennsylvania

The current form of Family Services of Western Pennsylvania was incorporated in 1948, however, the agency evolved from mergers of predecessor agencies that date back to 1885. The earliest parent of FSWP was the Western Pennsylvania Children's Aid Society, founded in 1885 to provide care for children who were abandoned, orphaned or unable to be cared for by their natural parents.

In essence, the agency created Western Pennsylvania's first Foster Care Program. Another early predecessor was the Civil Club, originally called the Child Labor Committee, formed to protect children from exploitation and to develop social resources for children in the community. This group merged into an agency named Associated Charities in 1908, and while aggressive in addressing the broader social issues that affected children in the early part of the century, formed its own Children's Bureau. Internal strife led Children's Bureau to split from Associated Charities in 1913 and join with the other children advocates in forming the Children's Aid Society of Allegheny County. Associated Charities became known informally as the Family Welfare Association, later as the Family Society and later as the Family Service Association.

It became an important provider of casework services during the Great Depression, and was involved in training people for the field of Social Work. In the early 1930's the agency joined with the Buhl Foundation and the Urban League in developing the School of Social Work at the University of Pittsburgh. The Children's Aid Society, Children's Bureau, and Associated Charities under its various names, operated separately through the various movements and developments in social services for children and families that occurred in the 1920'x, 1930's, and 1940's, until 1948, when they merged to form Family and Children's Services of Allegheny County, later renamed Family Services of Western Pennsylvania. In the early 1950'x, the agency focused on bringing stability into the lives of children and families through casework, homemaker services, foster care and adoption services. The 1952 Annual Report speaks of the agency's effort to turn "impossibilities into possibilities". This phrase became a theme of the document.

Charles Loring Brace
Founder of The Orphan Trains

Charles Loring Brace was born in Litchfield, Connecticut, June 19, 1826. He was educated for the clergy and ordained as a Methodist minister. But at age twenty-six he was asked to head up the newly formed Children's Aid Society of New York, which became his life ministry.

A true humanitarian, Rev. Brace walked the streets of New York that were swollen with successive tides of emigrants. His focus became the neglected "street children' and other children of poverty. Here he felt there was hope for redeeming young lives, their fate had not yet hardened. An astute social analyst as well, Brace believed addressing the needs of these thousands of street children was mandatory if society hoped to prevent a growing "dangerous class" of criminals sucking on society just to survive.

But Brace was against "charity" for its own sake. He believed that orphanages (and institutional life in general), and even "soup kitchens" that simply handed out meals, developed an unhealthy dependence on "Being done for" rather than "doing for oneself." All Brace's efforts - newsboy lodging houses, Sunday boys' meetings, industrial schools, night schools, and workshops - were efforts to help the young help themselves.

At this time in history, with westward expansion and the building of the railroads across the country, the primary mode of transporting children to the Midwest was by train. Thus the "orphan trains" were born, a systematic "placing out" of children that continued for almost seventy-five years. Though the plans had its critics and occasional failures, about two hundred thousand children were placed in families, most of whom grew up to become productive citizens. The Society made ever attempt to follow on the children they placed, and a report in 1910 said that eighty-seven percent were "doing well."

Charles Loring Brace was a prolific writer - of letters, pamphlets, articles, and books - and a tireless speaker on behalf of neglected children. His persuasive arguments won support from "the better classes" for his humanitarian efforts.

Though committed to his work in the city, Rev. Brace drew great inspiration and renewal from the country. He decided that city children could benefit from exposure to the country, as well. In 1875, a summer house was established where street children could spend a week in the fresh air by the sea. Later, after his death, the Brace Memorial Farm was established, where street children could not only learn farming skills, but manners and personal social skills to help prepare them for family life.

Charles Loring Brace died of Bright's disease on August 11, 1890, but his son, C.L. Brace, Jr., and other dedicated agents continue his work. The orphan train finally came to an end in the 1920's, as changing social attitudes about family focused on keeping families together, and changing laws helped curb child labor and established compulsory education.

But in the latter part of the nineteenth century, Charles Loring Brace and the Children's Aid Society of New York had worked tirelessly to save the lives of neglected children, most of whom became productive citizens.

Orphan Train States

Alabama, Arkansas, California, Colorado, Canada, Connecticut, Delaware, District of Columbia, Florida, Georgia, Idaho, Illinois, Indiana, Iowa, Kansas, Kentucky, Louisiana, Maine, Maryland, Massachusetts, Michigan, Minnesota, Mississippi, Missouri, Montana, Nebraska, Nevada, New Jersey, New York, New Mexico, North Carolina, North Dakota, Ohio, Oklahoma, Oregon, Pennsylvania, Rhode Island, South Carolina, South Dakota, Tennessee, Texas, Utah, Vermont, Virginia, Washington, West Virginia, Wisconsin, Wyoming

Riders On The Orphan Trains

By permission of Riders On The Orphan Trains Facebook site, I am able to share their story.
https://www.facebook.com/pages/Riders-on-the-Orphan-Train/153491214678718

The Children's Home of Pittsburgh and Lemieux Family Center

http://www.childrenshomepgh.org/lemicux-family-center

By permission of The Children's Home of Pittsburgh and Lemieux Family Center I wanted to share this site with you. I was overwhelmed by the love each worker there had for each child that entered the doors of this home. If you ever have the chance to visit, please do. It will change your life for the better.

Reference Material

While I was doing my research on Children's Homes, I came across a book by Reg Niles: Adoption Agencies, Orphanages and Maternity Homes: An Historical Directory Vol 1 & 2.

By permission of Reg Niles, here is the site:
http://www.triadoption.com/Reg%20Niles%20AAOMH.htm

Search and support directory:
http://www.triadoption.com/Search%20Support%20Directory.htm

Surname Birth date index: etc.
http://www.triadoption.com/Surname%20Birthdate.htm

Also by permission of Reg Niles is the Reg Niles Search book:
http://booklocker.com/books/6664.html

Pat Baer's Story

As told in Pat's own words:

To my friend Janet,

Allow me to share with you my memories concerning The Children's Home, 141 Oakland Ave., Uniontown, PA.
The first question one would ask? How did I get there? I was too young to understand WHY. But I was there not once, but twice and I remember being treated as a child that understood that "something was different". No Mama...No Pappa...No Uncles...No Aunts...Just a bunch of other "kids".
I'll start when I was six years old. I was enrolled in the first grade at a school named Boyle Elementary. We had a pet crow that would sit on your shoulder and talk to you. This is a fact. I also had a pet skunk that I fed bread crumbs each morning before trotting off to school. This too is a fact, and my little friend wasn't "fixed", if you know what I mean. Never experienced an accident.
My claim to fame was singing before the entire school on stage, the "Blue Birds of Dover".
Shortly thereafter, a woman I'll refer to as Ella, gave me a foster home that lasted five years. I was remanded to the Home for round number two.
They enrolled me in the Boy Scouts of America, which I thought was great, but this didn't last. I had to leave at the age of twelve. That was the rules. So I was off to another "School for Boys" in Pittsburgh. It was there that my attitude towards life started to change. My peers started to treat me as a person who was different.
Here we go again...No Mama...No Pappa...No nothing except my honor of which I defended with my fists. This continued right up to my day of graduation from high school.
In 1952 I enlisted in the USAF. Korea was a hot issue at that time, "Police Action". I landed there January 1954, 6 months after the cease fire.
I am retired and living on Long Island, NY. I don't plan to return to Uniontown. There were the good times...there were the bad times.. They say age and time heals all wounds. I'm still waiting.

Your friend Patrick

108

August 22, 2005

Mr. Patrick Baer,

The following information is being provided as per your request. This information was listed in the book that was kept by The Children's Aid Society, which no longer exists. Fayette County Children and Youth Services maintains their books.

Your name is listed as Newton Baer Smargie. You were born on April 4, 1933 in Masontown, PA. Your birth father was protestant and your birth mother was Greek Catholic. Your birth father is listed as G. Newton Baer age 32. Your birth mother is Rose Marie Smargie age 21. She was born in Martin, PA.

Your father was a farmer and lived near Masontown, PA. Your birth mother lived near Vanderbilt, PA. She reported to Children's Aid Society that she was unable to work and her parents would not permit for her to bring the baby home.

The Children's Aid Society placed you with Mr. and Mrs. James Gazelle on October 3, 1933 in Masontown, PA. On March 2, 1939, you were placed with The Children's Aid Society because the Gazells' were not getting along. You were then placed with Miss Ella McAndrews in Haddenville, PA on June 25, 1940 for the Summer. In August 1943, it was noted that Miss Andrews had moved to 59 Oakland Avenue, Uniontown, PA and that you were doing fine. Miss Andrews called and said she had secured the date of your baptism, which was May 18, 1933 for the Orthodox Greek Catholic Church, Masontown, PA. She also entered you into school as Newton Smargie Baer. Miss McAndrews had gone for treatment as she was not well, and had to return you to the home for awhile. She took you back with her on July 24, 1945. She and you returned you to the home on June 14, 1946. You were discharged from the home on June 21, 1946 and placed with Catholic Charities through a woman named Miss. Rush.

I hope this is helpful to you.

Sincerely

Singular Trip Taken by Little Mary Roman

Taken from The Herald Standard - November 26, 1921

How a tot scarcely four years old, walked a full seven miles, dodging freight trains and automobiles and traveling always in the general direction of her home near Flatwoods, was the remarkable story uncovered by Mrs. P.A. Johns, president of Children's Aid Society and Mrs. Mary Shaffer, Fayette County Red Cross nurse, as a result of their investigations concluded yesterday.

Last Tuesday, Mary Roman decided that she wanted to go home. She has been in The Children's Home on Oakland Avenue less then two months and became homesick. Mary will not be four years old until next February. When she informed the matron, Miss Anna Kuhns, that she was going home, Miss Kuhns said "all right", hardly dreaming that the tot would act on her word.

An hour later, Mary was missed. And then began the trace in which nurses, state police, and even the county detective were brought into play. Lots of people had seen Mary with her bright red riding cape as she made her way downtown. At first it was hard to believe that she left the city.

But to chronicle Mary's story as she tells it:

Down there (pointing to the P.R.R. Station) is where we got off when I came. I wanted to go home to see Mamma. Then I walked and walked and walked. Once a bad man's train came along (here Mary shook her little fist), but I got off the track. Nice man tell me where to go."

Mary describes her trip to Vance's Mill, and on toward Uppermiddletown. It was at the latter place that Mary, tired, her shoes almost worn out, but still ready to keep on. The foreman found a place for the child in Waltersburg that night and the next day, and the state police were notified and they in turn notified County Detective Russell. Between them all, they brought the tired little girl back to The Children's Home where a good warm meal and comfortable woolen blankets made the world appear roseate once more, and all her troubles were forgotten.

To cap Mary's successful adventure, members of the family, after hearing of the amazing trip, came down and gratified Mary's desire after all, by taking her home for a short stay. When Mary returns, she will be entirely satisfied with her new home and she will have accomplished something in the way of long distance hikes that is recorded of no other four year old in this vicinity.

At least that is the belief of Mrs. Johns and Miss Shaffer, who themselves covered the distance to Waltersburg just to prove to themselves that the little girl did it. Mary's mother is tubercular, and it was judged best to avoid exposing the children as much as possible. For that reason, the Red Cross and The Children's Home have taken a merciful hand.

110

Revisit to Children's Home - 2003 - photos

John (twin) and I

John's memories of almost 50 years
at The Children's Home 2003 at the Home

Boy's bathroom

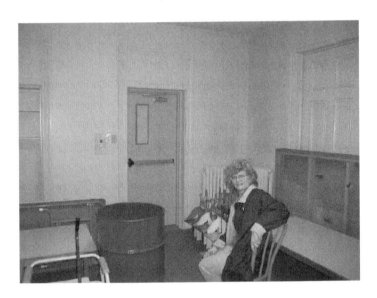

One of the large dining rooms

The original swing set I played on as a child

Side view of The Children's Home - 2003

113

Driveway to The Children's Home building - 2003

Yard of The Children's Home building - 2003

114

My revisit to the Children's Home Building - 2003

My Presentation on The Children's Home History Fayette County Genealogy Society

Lewana King, Me, Helen Fike

Side view of The Children's Home building - 2003

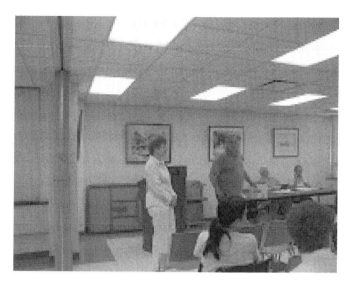

Getting ready for my presentation of The Children's Home history

Side view of The Children's Home

Driveway to The Children's Home

The Children's Home - 2005

118

Pat Trimble - president of The Fayette County Genealogy Society

The porch all along the front of the building is gone now. I still think and wonder about all the children that have graced the doors of the home and wondered how their lives have turned out. It was a very loving home for children. We were cared and loved just like a family. I thank God my biological mother placed me here to have a much better life than she could have ever given me. Her decision had changed my life forever.

Free Methodist Church, Uniontown, Pa

I attended The Free Methodist Church when I was in The Children's Home. When I returned to the church 50 years after leaving the home, I found a connection here. I was able to meet Pastor Eugene Cowsert and his wife Ida. I told Ida when we met ,you seem so familiar to me and she said the same thing to me. I had made a connection here. How interesting it was to hear of what Sunday School was like for me. Pastor Cowsert was pastoring when I attended in 1957-1958. What a joy it was to come back here and find my place. Free Methodist Church, 300 Evans St. Uniontown, PA

Lobby on first floor

Meeting area for church, first floor

Balcony, first floor

121

Pastor James Jobes

Free Methodist Church

122

Sunday School Room, basement

All ready for Sunday School

123

True Miracles With Genealogy - Roots Solved

Petition for Dissolving of The Children's Home

March 20, 1990

CHILDREN'S AID SOCIETY OF FAYETTE COUNTY,
IN THE COMMON PLEAS OF FAYETTE COUNTY
PENNSYLVANIA, ORPHANS COURT DIVISION.

CERTIFICATE

1.   The within Petition was filed by Coldren, Adams, Dehaas & Radcliffe on behalf of the Children's Aid Society of Fayette County, the moving party herein, on March 20, 1990.
2.   This petition will be presented in Motions Court on April 2, 1990, at 9:00 a.m.
3.   This Petition should be classified as a Routine Motion.
4.   No Judge has previously ruled on a related matter in this case.
5.   The citation for this Court's authority to grant the relief requested is as follows: Subsection 5547(b) of the Nonprofit Corporation Law of 1988 and by Section 6110 of the Probate, Estates and Fiduciaries Code.

COLDREN, ADAMS, DEHAAS & RADCLIFFE

PETITION

TO THE HONORABLE, THE PRESIDING JUDGE OF THE
SAID DIVISION

The petition of The Children's Aid Society of Fayette County
respectfully represents that:

1.   The petitioner is a non-profit corporation, organized as a
corporation of the first class under paragraph 2 of the Act of April
29, 1974. A copy of the petition for incorporation, dated April 8,
1919, and filed at No. 227 March Term 1919 in this court, is
attached hereto as Exhibit "A."

2.   The incorporation was approved by decree of this court on
May 6, 1919, a copy of which is attached hereto as Exhibit "B."

3.   The Charter of the petitioner was recorded in the Charter
Book No. 6, page 161, in the Office of the Recorder of Deeds of
Fayette County. A true and correct copy thereof is attached as
"Exhibit "C."

4.   Article second of the petitioner's Carter provides, "the said
corporation is formed for the purpose of providing for the welfare
of destitute and neglected children by such means as shall be best
for them and for the community by making for them a temporary
home until permanent homes may be secured; and to secure funds
for said purpose by donations and payments from parents and
guardians where the same are able to make payment and from other
sources and for said purpose to own, hold and to occupy real estate
but from which no profit shall be derived..."

5.   From 1886 to it's incorporation in 1919 the Society
provided shelter and care for nearly 900 neglected and destitute
children.

6.   In 1920, the petitioner acquired a large residence on
Oakland Avenue in Uniontown which the petitioner operated as
The Children's Home.

7.   From 1920 to 1958, The Children's Home was a sanctuary
for over 800 homeless children.

8.   After The Children's Home was closed in 1958, the petitioner continued to use its resources to care for the homeless children by providing for their needs and arranging for their care in private homes.

9.   Out of respect for the privacy of the children involved, the petitioner has never publicized the identity of the children to whom the petitioner offered care. Neither has the petitioner sought any public acclaim for its efforts.

10.   As times and habits have changed over the years, the need for a private institution to care for homeless children has diminished.

11.   During the past year, a final payment was made for the last of the children cared for by the petitioner.

12.   On February 7, 1990, the Board of Directors of the petitioner voted to dissolve the corporation. The members approved the dissolution at a meeting duly held on March 29,1990.

13.   Through the generosity of thoughtful persons in the Uniontown area, the petitioner has always had funds to provide for the care of the children trusted to it. As it nears its dissolution, the petitioner has on hand liquid assets in the amount of approximately $50,000.

14.   At their meeting on March 29, 1990, the members of the petitioner voted to ask the court to direct the following distribution of remaining funds.

Uniontown Public Library, for the use in the Children's program - 35%

Young Men's Christian Association of Uniontown for its Pool Project - 35%

Easter Seal Society - 10%

Westmoreland/Fayette Council, Boy Scouts of America, for use in the Uniontown Area - 5%

Girl Scouts of Southwestern Pennsylvania, for use in the Uniontown Area - 5%

Cities in Schools in Fayette County, Inc. - 10%

15.   The members of the petitioner believe that the suggested distribution of the remaining funds will meet the expectations of the founders of the petitioner and of the generous persons who have contributed to the petitioner.

16.   The relief requested by the petitioner is authorized by subsection 5547(b) of the Nonprofit Corporation Law of 1988 and by Section 6110 of the Probate, Estates and Fiduciaries Code.

COLDRAN, ADAMS, DEHAAS & RADCLIFF

Group for Children Dissolved by Court

Taken from the Herald Standard 04-20-1990

The Children's Aid society of Fayette County, which provided care for destitute children since 1919, has been dissolved by a recent Fayette County Court order.

Judge William J. Franks earlier this month approved a petition filed by the society, a non-profit corporation, at the request of its attorney Ira B. Coldren, Jr.

However, despite its dissolution, the corporation will benefit the area's children one last time.

Approximately $50,000, representing the corporation's remaining assets, will be divided among several area organizations, all involved in children's activities.

According to the petition, the Uniontown Public Library will receive thirty-five percent of the money for use in children's program.

The Young Men Christian Association of Uniontown (YMCA) also stands to receive thirty-five percent of the funds for its pool project.

The Easter Seal Society and the Cities in Schools in Fayette County, Inc. each will receive ten percent of the corporation's remaining funding.

And for use in the Uniontown area, the Westmoreland/Fayette Council, Boy Scouts of America and Girl Scouts of Western Pennsylvania each will receive five percent of the money.

Court records indicate that the corporation was recorded in the county in April 1919. It was formed for the "purpose of providing for the welfare of destitute and neglected children by such means as shall be best for them and the community."

The society located temporary homes for children until permanent homes could be secured, getting its funding from donations and payments from parents and guardians.

"Through the generosity of thoughtful persons in the Uniontown area the petitioner has always had funds to provide for the care of

128

children entrusted to it," the petition states.

From 1886 to its incorporation in 1919, the society provided shelter and care for nearly 900 neglected and destitute children.

A year after its incorporation, the society acquired a large residence on Oakland Avenue, for operation of its Children's Home.

From then until 1958, when the facility closed, the home provided care for over 800 children.

The petition notes that the society continued to care for children after closing the home by helping homeless children in providing for their needs and arranging for their care in private homes.

A final payment for the last of the children cared for by the society was made last year (1989), according to the petition.

For the privacy of the children involved, the children helped by the society have never been named publicly, the document states.

The decision to dissolve the corporation resulted from a vote by its board of directors in February. The members approved the move in March and directed distribution of the funding.

More Pictures and Documents
for The Children's Home Revisit

Speakers of The Children's Home of Uniontown
Lewana King, Janet Mancini, Helen Fike
County Genealogical Society Meeting 19 June 2005

Janet L. Mancini looks through pictures
holding the first picture of her birth mother

Jan 10, 2002 - my birthday. We met again after 47 years.
At The Children's Home
Catherine Holland, Janet, Helen Fike, Lewana King
These women worked at the Children's Home in Union town

The Following Pages Are Receipts
From The Children's Home

133

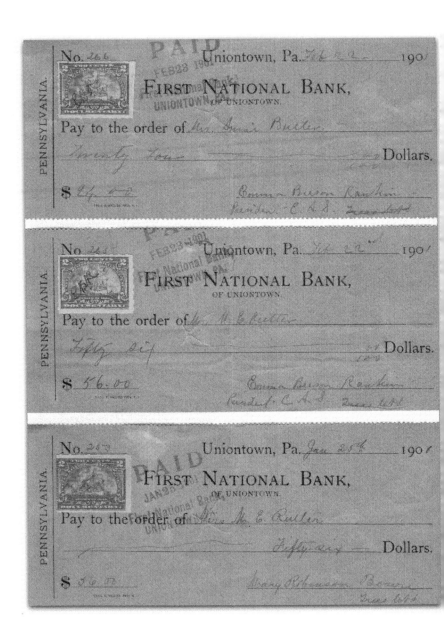

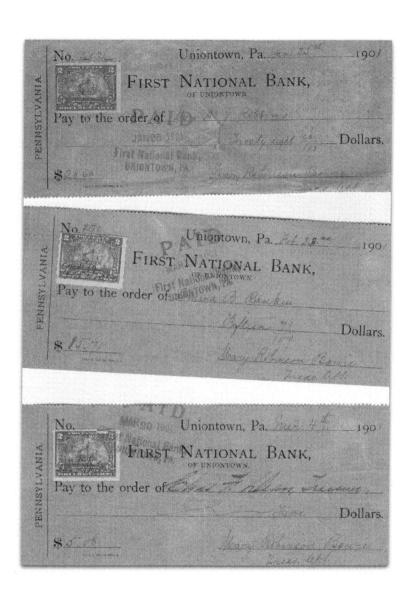

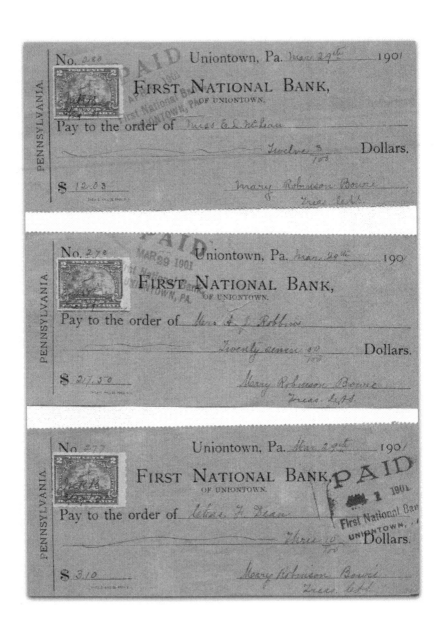

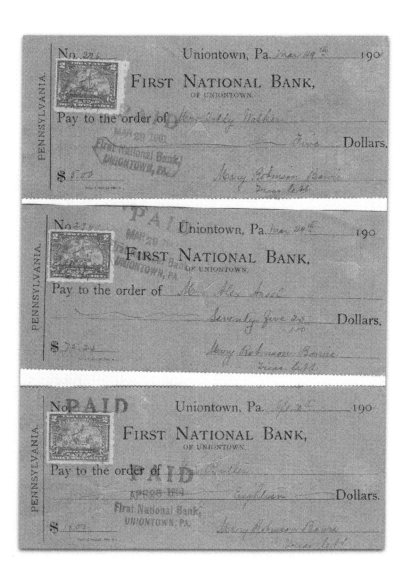

137

138

139

140

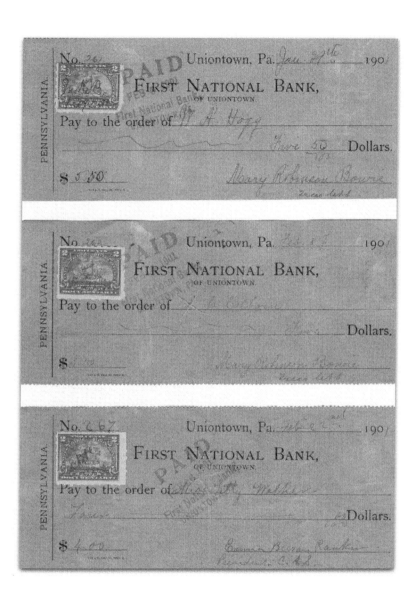

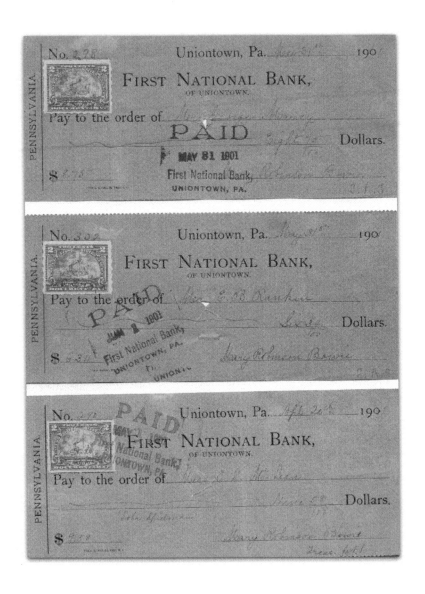

144

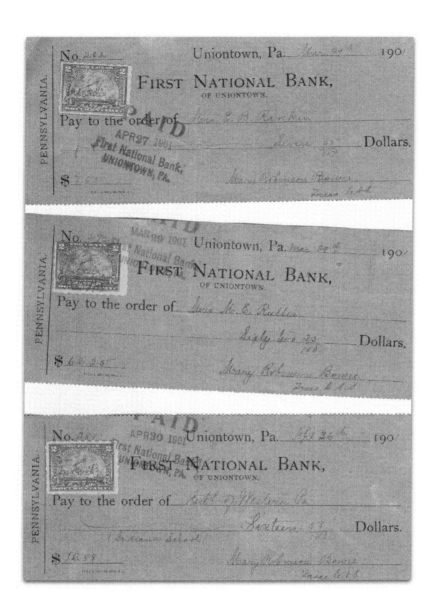

145

146

147

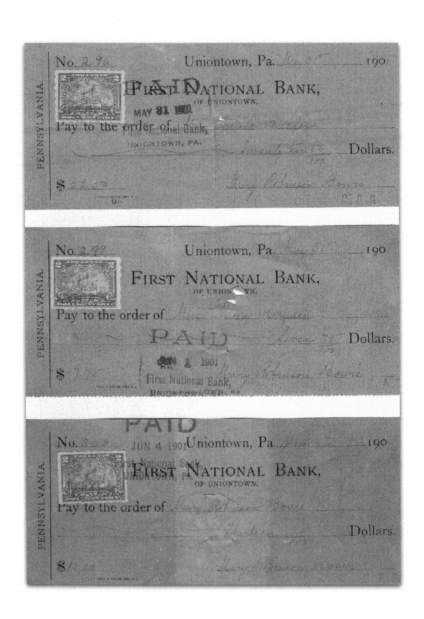

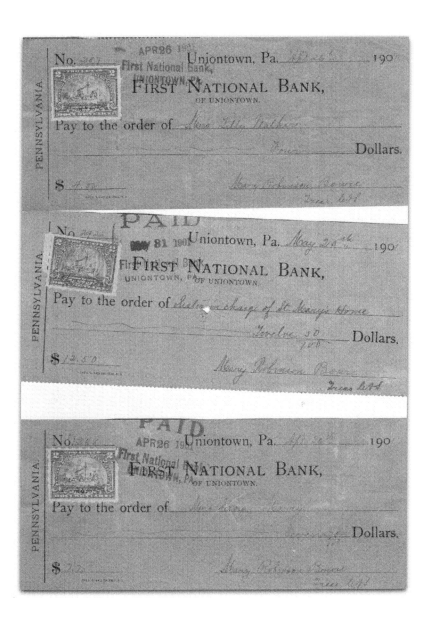

149

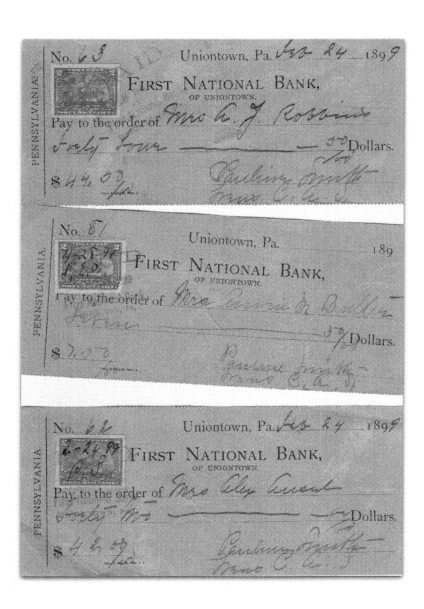

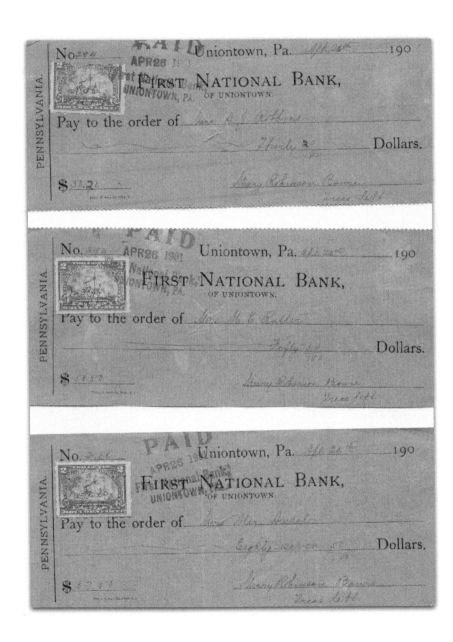

152

153

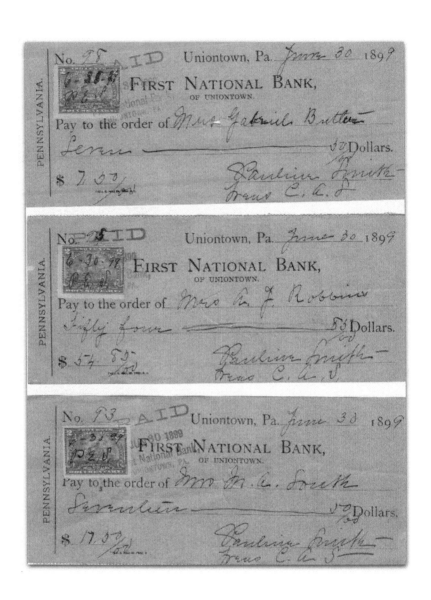

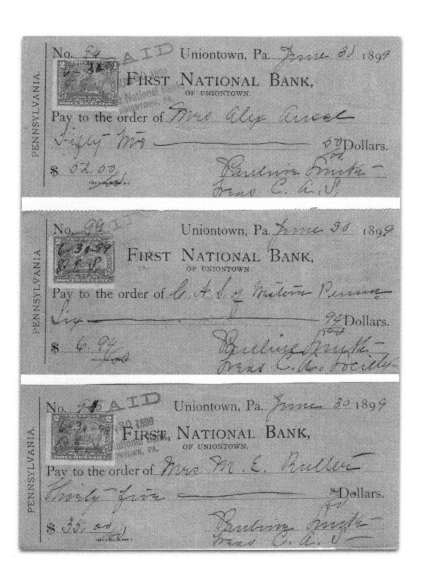

155

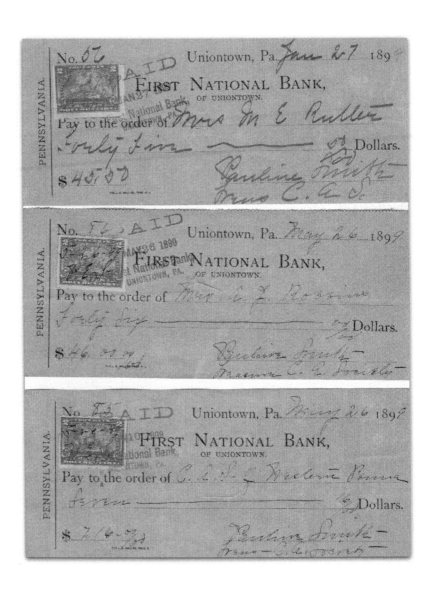

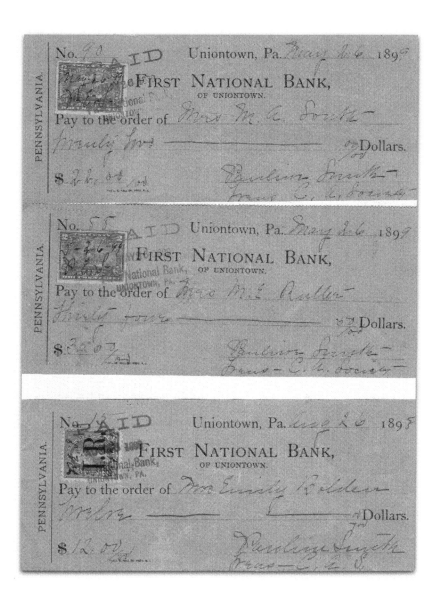

158

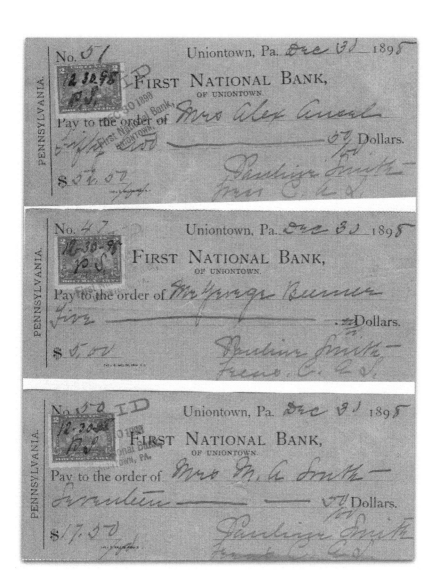

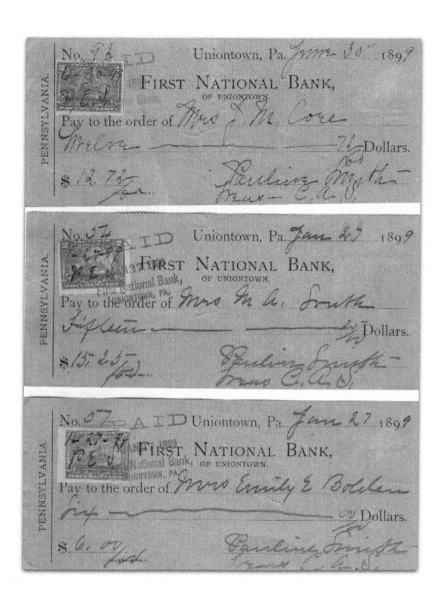

161

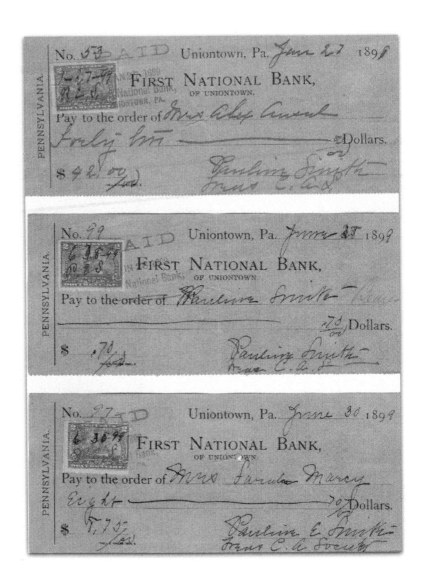

No. 53 · PAID · Uniontown, Pa. June 27 1898

PENNSYLVANIA

FIRST NATIONAL BANK,
OF UNIONTOWN.

Pay to the order of _____

Forty-two _____ Dollars.

$ 42 00/100

Pauline Smith
Treas. C. A. S.

No. 99 · PAID · Uniontown, Pa. June 28 1899

PENNSYLVANIA

FIRST NATIONAL BANK,
OF UNIONTOWN.

Pay to the order of _____

_____ 75/100 Dollars.

$ .75

Pauline Smith
Treas. C. A. S.

No. 27 · PAID · Uniontown, Pa. June 30 1899

PENNSYLVANIA

FIRST NATIONAL BANK,
OF UNIONTOWN.

Pay to the order of Mrs. Fannie Marcy

Eight _____ 70/100 Dollars.

$ 8,70

Pauline E. Smith
Treas. C. A. Society

162

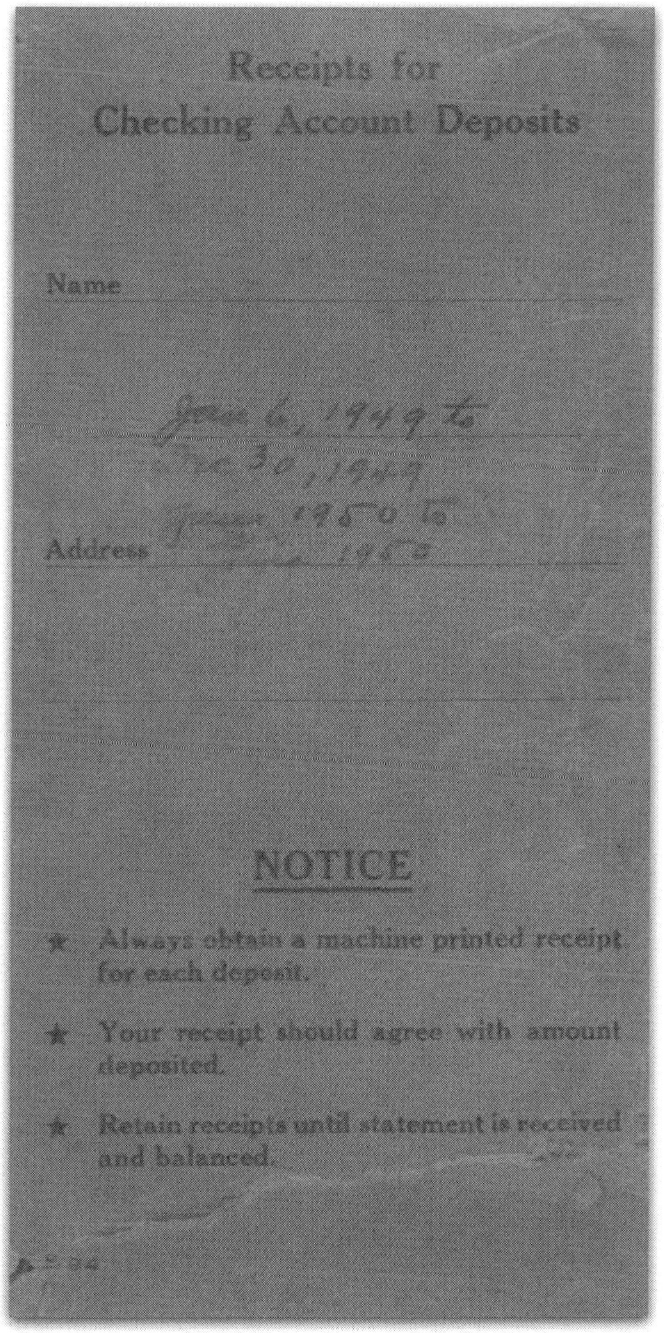

Receipts for
Checking Account Deposits

Name

June 6, 1949 to
Dec. 30, 1949
June 1950 to
Dec. 1950

Address

NOTICE

★ Always obtain a machine printed receipt for each deposit.

★ Your receipt should agree with amount deposited.

★ Retain receipts until statement is received and balanced.

163

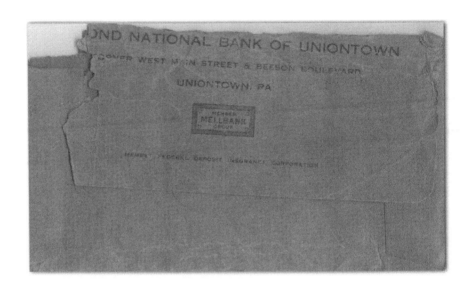

Definition of an Orphan - a child deprived by the death of one or usually both parents.

I was left an orphan after my biological mother, Mary Margaret Morris-Lener died in 1957. My father left; he did not want the responsibility of taking care of me or my younger siblings. But it was through my mother's love and choice that she placed me in The Children's Home.

In 2002, I decided to start my search for The Children's Home. I never would have imagined how my life has come full circle. I not only found The Children's Home, but my biological family also. This story is not only my story, but all those children that graced the doors of the home. We were placed there for various reasons, but it brought us together as a family.

Janet Louise Mancini can be contacted by email at:
oaklandave141@yahoo.com

Visit Janet L. Mancini's webpage 'Nobody's Child' at:
http://www.janetmancini.com/

Janet Louise Mancini

A great deal of thanks goes to Jan Abney, Editor and Author, who has made this come to pass. Her hard work has been beyond my expectations and made my dream come true for my book. Thank you from the bottom of my heart. I know it hasn't been easy.

Janet L. Mancine

Made in the USA
Charleston, SC
12 March 2014